World and the West

DATE DUE

DEMCO

THE WORLD
AND THE WEST

THE WORLD
AND THE WEST

BY
ARNOLD TOYNBEE

1953
OXFORD UNIVERSITY PRESS
NEW YORK AND LONDON

LITHOGRAPHED IN THE UNITED STATES OF AMERICA

PREFACE

THE encounter between the World and the West may well prove, in retrospect, to be the most important event in modern history. It is an outstanding instance of an historical phenomenon of which there are other famous instances in the past, and the comparative study of the course and consequences of these encounters between civilizations that are one another's contemporaries is one of the keys to an understanding of the history of mankind.

The present book reproduces, for a reader's eye, the Reith Lectures that were delivered by the author in the year 1952 on the invitation of the B.B.C. When the B.B.C. asked me to be their Reith Lecturer for that year, they suggested that I might offer for my subject one of the topics dealt with in the last four volumes of my book *A Study of History* which are now in the press and which are to be published in 1954. My choice was *The World and the West*; and, now that the Reith Lectures on this subject have been broadcast and been printed in current issues of *The Listener*, they have been collected for publication here in advance of the appearance of the remaining volumes of *A Study of History*.

The purpose of this book is to introduce, in a short and simple presentation, a subject that is dealt with on a so much larger scale in the forth-coming Volume VIII of *A Study of History* that the present treatment of it will not duplicate either the corresponding part of the *Study* (Volume VIII, Part IX) or, indeed, the corresponding passages of the single-volume abridgement of Volumes VII–X of the *Study* which Mr. D. C. Somervell is intending to make on the lines of his masterly abridgement of Volumes I–VI.

A.J.T.

December 1952

CONTENTS

I

RUSSIA AND THE WEST

PERHAPS the best way for the author to introduce a reader to the subject of this book will be to explain why he has given it the title that it bears. 'Why', the reader may be wondering, 'has the book been called "The World and the West"? Isn't the West just another name for as much of the world as has any importance for practical purposes today? And, if the author feels that he must say something about the non-Western rest of the world, why must he put the two words in this order? Why could he not write "The West and the World" instead of writing "The World and the West"? He might at least have put the West first.'

This title, as it stands, was chosen deliberately, in order to make two points that seem essential for an understanding of the subject. The first point is that the West has never been all of the world that matters. The West has not been the only actor on the stage of modern history even at the peak of the West's power (and this peak has perhaps now already been passed). The second point is this. In the encounter between the world and the West that has been going on by now for four or five hundred years, the world, not the West, is the party that, up to now, has had the significant experience. It has not been the West that has been hit by the world; it is the world that has been hit—and hit hard—by the West; and that is why, in the title of this book, the world has been put first.

A Westerner who wants to grapple with this subject, must try, for a few minutes, to slip out of his native Western skin and look at the encounter between the world and the West through the eyes of the great non-Western majority of mankind. Different though the non-Western peoples of the world may be from one another in race, language, civilization, and religion, if any Western inquirer asks them their opinion of the West, he will hear them all giving him the same answer: Russians, Muslims, Hindus, Chinese, Japanese, and all the rest. The West, they will tell him, has been the arch-aggressor of modern times, and each will have their own experience of Western aggression to bring up against him. The Russians will remind him that their country has been invaded by Western armies overland in 1941, 1915, 1812, 1709, and 1610; the peoples of Africa and Asia will remind him that Western missionaries, traders, and soldiers from across the sea have been pushing into their countries from the coasts since the fifteenth century. The Asians will also remind him that, within the same period, the Westerners have occupied the lion's share of the world's last vacant lands in the Americas, Australia, New Zealand, and South and East Africa. The Africans will remind him that they were enslaved and deported across the Atlantic in order to serve the European colonizers of the Americas as living tools to minister to their Western masters' greed for wealth. The descendants of the aboriginal population of North America will remind him that their ancestors were swept aside to make room for the West European intruders and for their African slaves.

This indictment will surprise, shock, grieve, and perhaps even outrage most Westerners today. Dutch Westerners are conscious of having evacuated Indonesia, and British Westerners of having evacuated India, Pakistan, Burma, and Ceylon, since 1945. British Westerners have no aggressive war on their consciences since the South African War of 1899–1902, and American Westerners none since the Spanish-American War of 1898. We forget all too easily that the Germans, who attacked their neighbours, including Russia, in the First World War and again in the Second World War, are Westerners too, and that the Russians, Asians, and Africans do not draw fine distinctions between different hordes of 'Franks'—which is the world's common name for Westerners in the mass. 'When the world passes judgement, it can be sure of having the last word', according to a well-known Latin proverb. And certainly the world's judgement on the West does seem to be justified over a period of about four and a half centuries ending in 1945. In the world's experience of the West during all that time, the West has been the aggressor on the whole; and, if the tables are being turned on the West by Russia and China today, this is a new chapter of the story which did not begin until after the end of the Second World War. The West's alarm and anger at recent acts of Russian and Chinese aggression at the West's expense are evidence that, for us Westerners, it is today still a strange experience to be suffering at the hands of the world what the world has been suffering at Western hands for a number of centuries past.

What, then, has been the world's experience of the West? Let us begin with Russia's experience, for Russia is part of the world's great non-Western majority. Though the Russians have been Christians and are, many of them, Christians still, they have never been Western Christians. Russia was converted not from Rome, as England was, but from Constantinople; and, in spite of their common Christian origins, Eastern and Western Christendom have always been foreign to one another, and have often been mutually antipathetic and hostile, as Russia and the West unhappily still are today, when each of them is in what one might call a 'post-Christian' phase of its history.

This on the whole unhappy story of Russia's relations with the West did, though, have a happier first chapter; for, in spite of the difference between the Russian and the Western way of life, Russia and the West got on fairly well with one another in the early Middle Ages. The peoples traded, and the royal families intermarried. An English King Harold's daughter, for instance, married a Russian prince. The estrangement began in the thirteenth century, after the subjugation of Russia by the Tatars. The Tatars' domination over Russia was temporary, because the Tatars were Nomads from the Steppes who could not ever make themselves at home in Russia's fields and forests. Russia's lasting losses as a result of this temporary Tatar conquest were, not to her Tatar conquerors, but to her Western neighbours; for these took advantage of Russia's prostration in order to lop off, and annex to Western Christendom, the western fringes of the Russian world in White Russia and in the western half of the Ukraine. It was not till 1945 that Russia recaptured the last piece of these huge Russian territories that were taken from her by Western Powers in the thirteenth and fourteenth centuries.

These Western conquests at Russia's expense in the late Middle Ages had an effect on Russia's life at home, as well as on her relations with her Western assailants. The pressure on Russia from the West did not merely estrange Russia from the West; it was one of the hard facts of Russian life that moved the Russians to submit to the yoke of a new native Russian Power at Moscow which, at the price of autocracy, imposed on Russia the political unity that she now had to have if she was to survive. It was no accident that this new-fangled autocratic centralizing government of Russia should have arisen at Moscow; for Moscow stood in the fairway of the easiest line for the invasion of what was left of Russia by a Western aggressor. The Poles in 1610, the French in 1812, the Germans in 1941, all marched this way. Since an early date in the fourteenth century, autocracy and centralization have been the dominant notes of all successive Russian régimes. This Muscovite Russian political tradition has perhaps always been as disagreeable for the Russians themselves as it has certainly been distasteful and alarming to their neighbours; but unfortunately the Russians have learnt to put up with it, partly perhaps out of sheer habit, but also, no doubt, because they have felt it to be a lesser evil than the alternative fate of being conquered by aggressive neighbours.

This Russian attitude of resignation towards an autocratic régime that has become traditional in Russia is, of course, one of the main difficulties, as we Westerners see it, in the relations between Russia and the West today. The great majority of people in the West feel that tyranny is an intolerable social evil. At a fearful cost we have put down tyranny when it has raised its head among our Western selves in the forms of Fascism and National Socialism. We feel the same detestation and distrust of it in its Russian form, whether this calls itself Czarism or calls itself Communism. We do not want to see this Russian brand of tyranny spread; and we are particularly concerned about this danger to Western ideals of liberty now that we Franks find ourselves thrown upon the defensive for the first time in our history since the second Turkish siege of Vienna in 1682–3. Our present anxiety about what seems to us to be a post-war threat to the West from Russia is a well-justified anxiety in our belief. At the same time, we must take care not to allow the reversal in the relation between Russia and the West since 1945 to mislead us into forgetting the past in our natural preoccupation with the present. When we look at the encounter between Russia and the West in the historian's instead of the journalist's perspective, we shall see that, over a period of several centuries ending in 1945, the Russians have had the same reason for looking askance at the West that we Westerners feel that we have for looking askance at Russia today.

During the last few centuries, this threat to Russia from the West, which has been a constant threat from the thirteenth century till 1945, has been made more serious for Russia by the outbreak, in the West, of a technological revolution which has become chronic and which does not yet show any signs of abating.

When the West adopted fire-arms, Russia followed suit, and in the sixteenth century she used these new weapons from the West to conquer the Tatars in the Volga valley and more primitive peoples in the Urals and in Siberia. But in 1610 the superiority of the Western armaments of the day enabled the Poles to occupy Moscow and to hold it for two years, while at about the same time the Swedes were also able to deprive Russia of her outlet on the Baltic Sea at the head of the Gulf of Finland. The Russian retort to these seventeenth-century Western acts of aggression was to adopt the technology of the West wholesale, together with as much of the Western way of life as was inseparable from Western technology.

It was characteristic of the autocratic centralizing Muscovite régime that this technological and accompanying social revolution in Russia at the turn of the seventeenth and eighteenth centuries should have been imposed upon Russia from above downwards, by the fiat of one man of genius, Peter the Great. Peter is a key figure for an understanding of the world's relations with the West not only in Russia but everywhere; for Peter is the archetype of the autocratic Westernizing reformer who, during the last two and a half centuries, has saved

the world from falling entirely under Western
domination by forcing the world to train itself to
resist Western aggression with Western weapons.
Sultans Selīm III and Mahmūd II and President
Mustafā Kemāl Atatürk in Turkey, Mehmed 'Alī
Pasha in Egypt, and 'the Elder Statesmen', who
made the Westernizing revolution in Japan in the
eighteen-sixties, were, all of them, following in
Peter the Great's footsteps consciously or uncon-
sciously.

Peter launched Russia on a technological race
with the West which Russia is still running. Russia
has never yet been able to afford to rest, because
the West has continually been making fresh spurts.
For example, Peter and his eighteenth-century
successors brought Russia close enough abreast of
the Western world of the day to make Russia just
able to defeat her Swedish Western invaders in
1709 and her French Western invaders in 1812;
but, in the nineteenth-century Western industrial
revolution, the West once more left Russia behind,
so that in the First World War Russia was defeated
by her German Western invaders as she had been
defeated, two hundred years earlier, by the Poles
and the Swedes. The present Communist autocratic government was able to supplant the Czar-
dom in Russia in consequence of Russia's defeat
by an industrial Western technology in 1914–17;
and the Communist régime then set out, from 1928

to 1941, to do for Russia, all over again, what the Czar Peter had done for her about 230 years earlier.

For the second time in the modern chapter of her history Russia was now put, by an autocratic ruler, through a forced march to catch up with a Western technology that had once more shot ahead of hers; and Stalin's tyrannical course of technological Westernization was eventually justified, like Peter's, through an ordeal by battle. The Communist technological revolution in Russia defeated the German invaders in the Second World War, as Peter's technological revolution had defeated the Swedish invaders in 1709 and the French invaders in 1812. And then, a few months after the completion of the liberation of Russian soil from German Western occupation in 1945, Russia's American Western allies dropped in Japan an atom bomb that announced the outbreak of a third Western technological revolution. So today, for the third time, Russia is having to make a forced march in an effort to catch up with a Western technology that, for the third time, has left her behind by shooting ahead. The result of this third event in the perpetual competition between Russia and the West still lies hidden in the future; but it is already clear that this renewal of the technological race is another of the very serious difficulties now besetting the relations between these two ex-Christian societies.

Technology is, of course, only a long Greek name for a bag of tools; and we have to ask ourselves: What are the tools that count in this competition in the use of tools as means to power? A power-loom or a locomotive is obviously a tool for this purpose, as well as a gun, an aeroplane, or a bomb. But all tools are not of the material kind; there are spiritual tools as well, and these are the most potent that Man has made. A creed, for instance, can be a tool; and, in the new round in the competition between Russia and the West that began in 1917, the Russians this time threw into their scale of the balances a creed that weighed as heavily against their Western competitors' material tools as, in the Roman story of the ransoming of Rome from the Gauls, the sword thrown in by Brennus weighed against the Roman gold.

Communism, then, is a weapon; and, like bombs, aeroplanes, and guns, this is a weapon of Western origin. If it had not been invented by a couple of nineteenth-century Westerners, Karl Marx and Friedrich Engels, who were brought up in the Rhineland and spent the best part of their working lives in London and in Manchester respectively, Communism could never have become Russia's official ideology. There was nothing in the Russian tradition that could have led the Russians to invent Communism for themselves; and it is certain that they would never have dreamed of it if it had not been lying, ready-made, there in the West, for a revolutionary Russian régime to apply in Russia in 1917.

In borrowing from the West a Western ideology, besides a Western industrial revolution, to serve as an anti-Western weapon, the Bolsheviki in 1917 were making a great new departure in Russian history; for this was the first time that Russia had ever borrowed a creed from the West. We have already noticed that Christianity had come to Russia, not from the West, but from Byzantium, where Christianity had a distinctive, non-Western form and spirit; and a fifteenth-century Western attempt to impose Western Christianity on Russia had been a failure. In A.D. 1439, at an ecclesiastical council held at Florence, representatives of the Eastern Orthodox Church in what then still remained of the Byzantine Empire had unwillingly recognized the ecclesiastical supremacy of the Roman See in the hope that, in return, the Western world would save Constantinople from conquest by the Turks. The metropolitan archbishop of Moscow, who was a suffragan of the Greek Patriarch of Constantinople, had been attending the council, and he had voted the same way as his brethren who were representing the Greek Orthodox Church; but, when he came home to Moscow, his recognition of the Pope's supremacy was repudiated there and he himself was deposed.

Two hundred and fifty years later, when Peter the Great went to the West to learn the 'know-how' of Western technology, there was no longer any question of Russia's being required to adopt a Western form of Christianity as the price of being initiated into the secrets of Western technological efficiency. Before the end of the seventeenth century there had been a revulsion in the West, not merely against religious fanaticism, but against religion itself, in consequence of the West's weariness of its own domestic wars of religion. The Western world, whose apprentice Russia became in Peter's day, was thus an irreligious world, and the sophisticated minority of Russians who became the agents of the Westernization of Russia followed the example of their sophisticated Western contemporaries by turning lukewarm towards the Russian form of Christianity without adopting any Western form of Christianity instead. So, in adopting Communism in 1917, Russia was making a breach with her traditions by taking up a Western creed for the first time in her history.

The reader will also have noticed that this Western creed, which Russia did take up in 1917, was one that was particularly well suited to serve Russia as a Western weapon for waging an anti-Western spiritual warfare. In the West, where Communism had arisen, this new creed was a heresy. It was a Western criticism of the West's failure to live up to her own Christian principles in the economic and social life of this professedly Christian society; and a creed of Western origin which was at the same time an indictment of Western practice was, of course, just the spiritual weapon that an adversary of the West would like to pick up and turn against its makers. With this Western spiritual weapon in her hands, Russia could carry her war with the West into the enemy's country on the spiritual plane. Since Communism had originated as a product of uneasy Western consciences, it could appeal to other uneasy Western consciences when it was radiated back into the Western world by a Russian propaganda. And so now, for the first time in the modern Western world's history since the close of the seventeenth century, when the flow of Western converts to Islam almost ceased, the West has again found itself threatened with spiritual disintegration from inside, as well as with an assault from outside. In thus threatening to undermine the Western civilization's foundations on the West's own home ground, Communism has already proved itself a more effective anti-Western weapon in Russian hands than any material weapon could ever be.

Communism has also served Russia as a weapon for bringing into the Russian camp the Chinese quarter of the human race, as well as other sections of that majority of mankind that is neither Russian nor Western. We know that the outcome of the struggle to win the allegiance of these neutrals may be decisive for the outcome of the Russo-Western conflict as a whole, because this non-Western and non-Russian majority of mankind may prove to hold the casting vote in a competition between Russia and the West for world power. Now Communism can make a twofold appeal to a depressed Asian, African, and Latin American peasantry when it is the voice of Russia that is commending Communism to them. The Russian spokesman can say to the Asian peasantry first: 'If you follow the Russian example, Communism will give you the strength to stand up against the West, as a Communist Russia can already stand up against the West today.' The second appeal of Communism to the Asian peasantry is Communism's claim that it can, and that private enterprise neither can nor would if it could, get rid of the extreme inequality between a rich minority and a poverty-stricken majority in Asian countries. Discontented Asians, however, are not the only public for whom Communism has an appeal. Communism also has an appeal for all men, since it can claim to offer mankind the unity which is our only alternative to self-destruction in an atomic age.

It looks as if, in the encounter between Russia and the West, the spiritual initiative, though not the technological lead, has now passed, at any rate for the moment, from the Western to the Russian side. We Westerners cannot afford to resign ourselves to this, because this Western heresy—Communism—which the Russians have taken up, seems to the great majority of people in the West to be a perverse, misguided, and disastrous doctrine and way of life. A theologian might put it that our great modern Western heresiarch Karl Marx has made what is a heretic's characteristic intellectual mistake and moral aberration. In putting his finger on one point in orthodox practice in which there has been a crying need for reform, he had lost sight of all other considerations and therefore has produced a remedy that is worse than the disease.

The Russians' recent success in capturing the initiative from us Westerners by taking up this Western heresy called Communism and radiating it out into the world in a cloud of anti-Western poison-gas does not, of course, mean that Communism is destined to prevail. Marx's vision seems, in non-Marxian eyes, far too narrow and too badly warped to be likely to prove permanently satisfying to human hearts and minds. All the same, Communism's success, so far as it has gone, looks like a portent of things to come. What it does tell us is that the present encounter between the world and the West is now moving off the technological plane on to the spiritual plane. Some light on this next chapter of the story, which for us still lies in the future, may be found in the history of the world's earlier encounter with Greece and Rome. But, before looking at that, we have to see how Islam, India, and the Far East have been faring in their present encounters with both the West and Russia.

II

ISLAM AND THE WEST

In the first chapter, two points have been made about Russia's encounter with the West: the first is that Russia has managed to hold her own against the West by adopting Western weapons; the second point is that one of these Western weapons adopted by Russia has been a creed, and that, through her adoption of this Western creed of Communism, Russia has been able to pass over from the defensive into the counter-offensive that is causing so much concern to us in the West today. This story of Russia's relations with our Western Society within our own lifetime is in some points a repetition of an older story, in which the modern Western civilization's part was played by its predecessor the Graeco-Roman civilization, and Russia's part was played by Islam.

Communism has been called a Christian heresy, and the same description applies to Islam as well. Islam, like Communism, won its way as a programme of reform for dealing with abuses in the contemporary practice of Christianity. And the success of Islam in its early days shows how powerful the appeal of a reforming heresy can be when the orthodoxy that this heresy is attacking is reluctant to mend its ways. In the seventh century of the Christian Era the Muslim Arabs liberated from a Christian Graeco-Roman ascendancy a string of Oriental countries—from Syria right across North Africa to Spain—which had been under Greek or Roman rule for nearly a thousand years—ever since Alexander the Great had conquered the Persian Empire and the Romans had overthrown Carthage. After that, between the eleventh century and the sixteenth, the Muslims went on to conquer, by stages, almost the whole of India, and their religion spread peacefully still farther afield: into Indonesia and China on the east and into Tropical Africa on the south-west. Russia too, as we have seen, was temporarily subject, in the Later Middle Ages, to Tatars who became converts to Islam, and all the rest of Eastern Orthodox Christendom, in Asia Minor and in South-Eastern Europe, was conquered in the fourteenth and fifteenth centuries by the Muslim Ottoman Turks. Vienna was besieged by the Turks for the second time no longer ago than 1682–3; and, though the failure of that siege marked the beginning of a turn of the tide in favour of the West in the West's encounter with an aggressive Ottoman Empire, the crescent flag could be seen still flying over the east coast of the Adriatic, opposite the heel of Italy, no longer ago than 1912.

Those tremendous military and political successes in the earlier chapters of the history of Islam explain why it was that the Turks and other Muslim peoples were so slow in following Peter the Great's policy of holding one's own against the West by adopting Western weapons, tools, institutions, and ideas. The technological Westernization of Russia by Peter the Great started less than a hundred years after Russia had had the experience of seeing Moscow occupied by Polish Western invaders in 1610–12. On the other hand, more than a hundred years passed after the Turkish disaster at Vienna in 1683 before a Turkish Sultan took the first step towards training Turkish infantry on a Western model, and 236 years passed before a Turkish statesman fired his countrymen to adopt the Western way of life whole-heartedly and without any reservations.

The military reforms initiated by Sultan Selīm III, who came to the throne in 1789, were prompted by the shock of Turkey's defeat by Russia in the Great Russo-Turkish War of 1768–74. Till then, the Turks had thought of the Russians as country cousins of the Turks' own despised Eastern Orthodox Christian Greek and Bulgarian subjects; and now the Turks had suffered a crushing defeat at these rustic Russians' hands because the Russians had mastered the Western military technique. As for the out-and-out Westernizing movement, which was launched by Mustafā Kemāl Atatürk in 1919, we may doubt whether even Atatürk's imaginative insight and demonic driving-power would have succeeded in jolting the Turks out of an age-old conservatism if, after the First World War, the Turks had not found themselves confronted with a stark and inescapable choice between whole-hearted Westernization and outright extinction.

The fact is that the Western counter-attack on the Islamic world, which, after the Turks' failure at Vienna in 1683, was bound to come sooner or later, was delayed by long Western memories of the Turks' and other Muslim peoples' historic military prowess. The Western world's retort to the Turks' conquest of Eastern Orthodox Christendom in the fourteenth and fifteenth centuries had been, not to make a fresh frontal attack on the Islamic world on the lines of the disastrously unsuccessful crusades, but to encircle Islam by conquering the Ocean. The circumnavigation of Africa had brought Portuguese Western seafarers to the west coast of India some years before the Mughals, who were the last wave of the Muslim invaders of India, came in by land from central Asia. The transit of the Atlantic Ocean and the Pacific Ocean, via Mexico, by the Spaniards, opened up in the Philippine Islands a new East Asian frontier between a Western Christendom and an Islam who had been neighbours, hitherto, only on the opposite side of the globe: in the

Danube valley and in the western Mediterranean. Indeed, before the end of the sixteenth century, the West, thanks to its conquest of the Ocean, had succeeded in throwing a lasso round Islam's neck; but it was not till the nineteenth century that the West ventured to pull the rope tight. Till as late as that, enduring memories, on both sides, of past Muslim military prowess kept the Westerners cautious and the Muslims self-complacent.

The experience that did slowly break the spell of this Muslim self-complacency was the repeated military defeat of the Ottoman Empire and other Muslim Powers by adversaries equipped with Western weapons and with the technology and the science that are the sinews of the modern Western art of war; and the Muslims' reaction to this experience was the same as the Russians'.

In Turkey from 1789 to 1919, as in Russia from 1699 to 1825, the typical revolutionary Westernizer was a young military or naval officer; and to Western minds this is surprising, because, in a Western country, the corps of professional officers in the fighting services is apt to be, not a hot-bed of revolution, but a stronghold of conservatism. Yet the facts are indisputable. In Russia, the Westernizing Czar Peter the Great's most effective agents for the execution of his revolutionary programme were his young guards officers; and, more than a hundred years after Peter's day, the planners of the unsuccessful revolution of 1825 against the conservative Czar Nicholas I were, once again, military officers who had been infected with the Western political ideas of the day in 1814, when they had been serving in the international army of occupation in France. In the nineteenth century one of the typical careers of a Russian revolutionary prophet or leader was to be born the son of a well-to-do landowner, to enter the military or civil service, to publish philosophizing articles in a literary magazine, to retire at an early age from the imperial service, and to spend the rest of his life living as a rentier and serving the cause of political and social reform in Russia on Westernizing lines. In Turkey it was in essence the same story. The unsuccessful pioneer Westernizer Sultan Selīm III, and his more effective successor Mahmūd II, both started by building up Western-trained military units; and in the Turkish revolution of 1908, which was a successful counterpart of the unsuccessful Russian revolution of 1825, young military officers were the moving spirits.

In the Turkish case, the reason for the prominence of young officers in the Westernizing movement is obvious. The purpose of the Turkish revolution of 1908 was to re-establish the Westernizing parliamentary Turkish constitution of 1876, which had been almost immediately set on one

side by the reactionary Sultan 'Abd-al-Hamīd II.
'Abd-al-Hamīd's political strategy, during his
thirty years of absolute government, for making
sure that Western Liberalism should never raise
its head again in Turkey, had been to suppress all
forms of 'dangerous thought'. Under his régime
there was a severe censorship of books and control
of education; but the one exception to 'Abd-al-
Hamīd's systematically obscurantist rule was the
education of the cadets for the professional fighting
services. 'Abd-al-Hamīd was morbidly afraid of
revolution, but at the same time he had the wit to
realize that he would lose his empire in another
way—through conquest by some militarily efficient foreign power—if he were to make it impossible for Turkish military cadets to keep abreast
of the progress of Western military science. He
tried, of course, to keep these Turkish cadets'
Western education within the narrowest possible
professional limits; but, when once these young
Turks had been allowed to learn Western languages in order to study Western military text-
books, it proved impossible to keep their minds in-
sulated from Western political ideas. The military
cadets were thus the one class in Hamidian Turkey
that was able to keep a mental window open to
influences from the West; and this is why in 1908,
after thirty years of an obscurantist despotic
régime, the spearhead of a fresh attack of Western

Liberalism in Turkey was the younger generation in the corps of military officers.

The necessity for Westernizing the Turkish army, which was thus admitted even by so extreme a reactionary as Sultan 'Abd-al-Hamīd II, had been recognized, as has been mentioned, a hundred years before this tyrant's time, by his unfortunate liberal-minded predecessor Selīm III. But, in this first chapter of the story, even the convinced Westernizers in Turkey had, at heart, no love for the alien Western civilization that they were deliberately introducing. Their intention was to take just the minimum dose of Western culture that was calculated to keep 'the sick man of Europe' alive; and this grudging spirit caused one instalment of Westernizing reforms in Turkey after another to miscarry. The verdict of history on this old school of Turkish Westernizers is 'Every time too little and too late'. They hoped to make Turkey able to hold her own in wars with Western Powers like Austria or Westernizing Powers like Russia just by putting Western uniforms on Turkish soldiers' bodies and Western weapons in their hands, and by giving Turkish officers a Western professional training. They wanted to keep all the rest of Turkish life on its traditional Islamic basis. The reason why this policy of a minimum dose of Westernization failed, and was bound to fail, was because it flew in the face of a truth to which these early Turkish military reformers were blind—though Peter the Great had shown his genius by perceiving it. This truth was that any civilization, any way of life, is an indivisible whole in which all the parts hang together and are interdependent.

For example, the secret of the West's superiority to the rest of the world in the art of war from the seventeenth century onwards is not to be found just in Western weapons, drill, and military training. It is not even to be found just in the civilian technology that supplies the military equipment. It cannot be understood without also taking into account the whole mind and soul of the Western Society of the day; and the truth is that the Western art of war has always been one facet of the Western way of life. Hence, an alien society that tried to acquire the art without attempting to live the life was bound to fail to master the art; while, conversely, a Russian, Turkish, or other non-Western military officer who did succeed in his profession up to the normal Western standard could achieve this only by acquiring much more of the Western civilization than was to be found in the textbook or on the parade-ground. In fact, the long-sought minimum solution of Turkey's ever more insistent 'Western Question' was no solution at all, and there were two practical alternative endings to the story: in the end, the Turks would either pay for their mistake of taking

minimum doses of the Western civilization by
going under, or else save themselves from extinction by Westernizing with all their heart and
mind and soul and strength. After they had
brought themselves to the verge of destruction by
taking the former of these two courses, they did
just save themselves by plunging, before it was too
late, into a course of unlimited Westernization
under the leadership of Mustafā Kemāl Atatürk.

Mustafā Kemāl was one of those young officers
who had imbibed Western ideas in the process of
receiving a Western professional military education in the last days of the Hamidian régime; and
he had then taken an active part in the Revolution
of 1908. Mustafā Kemāl's chance came when
Turkey was down and out in consequence of having shared her ally Germany's defeat in the First
World War. Kemāl had the wit to see that half-
measures of Westernization, which had always
been disastrous for Turkey, would be fatal for her
now; and he also had the character to move his
countrymen to follow his lead. Mustafā Kemāl's
policy was to aim at nothing short of an out-and-
out conversion of Turkey to the Western way of
life; and in the nineteen-twenties he put through
in Turkey what was perhaps as revolutionary a
programme as has ever been carried out in any
country deliberately and systematically in so short
a span of time. It was as if, in our Western world,

the Renaissance, the Reformation, the secularist scientific mental revolution at the end of the seventeenth century, the French Revolution, and the Industrial Revolution had all been telescoped into a single lifetime and been made compulsory by law. In Turkey the emancipation of women, the disestablishment of the Islamic religion, and the substitution of the Latin alphabet for the Arabic alphabet as the script for conveying the Turkish language were all enacted between 1922 and 1928.

This revolution was carried out by a dictator working through a single party enjoying a monopoly of power, and probably so much could not have been done so quickly by any less high-handed method. In the nineteen-twenties Turkey had either to turn her life inside out or else to perish, and the Turkish people chose to survive at all costs. One of the costs was a period of submission to a régime of the Fascist-Nazi-Communist type —though, in Turkey, the dictatorial institution of single-party government was never carried to totalitarian extremes. The sequel, though, is impressive and promising. In the Turkish general election of 1950, Turkey moved from a one-party to a two-party régime by consent, without violence or bloodshed. The party that had for so long held a monopoly of office now accepted the will of the electors, first by letting them vote freely, and secondly by taking the adverse vote as a signal for the hitherto dominant party to retire from office and let the Opposition take the Government over; and the Opposition, on their side, showed the same constitutional spirit. When they found themselves in power, they did not abuse their power by taking any vindictive measures against opponents who had respected the results of a free election by voluntarily making way for the victors at the polls.

It looks as if in Turkey, whose statesmen had tried for so many generations to 'make do' with the Western art of war alone, the Western institution of parliamentary constitutional government, which is so much nearer than our art of war is to the heart of our Western civilization, had now genuinely taken root. If so, this is a notable triumph for a sense of fair play and moderation in politics which, we Westerners believe, is one of the good gifts that the West is able to give to the world. Since 1917 we have seen many partially or nominally democratic peoples lapsing into divers forms of tyrannical government, and some of these peoples—for instance the Italians and the Germans—have been, not recent proselytes to our Western civilization, but native-born members of our Western family. The victory of the Western constitutional spirit in the Turkish elections of 1950 is thus a landmark which may perhaps even signify a turn of the political tide in the world as a whole.

There are, of course, other Western ideas and institutions which are doubtful blessings; and one of these is our Western Nationalism. The Turks, and many other Islamic peoples with them, have become as strongly infected with Nationalism as with other Western notions, salutary or pernicious. And we have to ask ourselves what is going to be the consequence of the intrusion of this narrow-hearted Western political ideal into an Islamic world whose own ancestral tradition is that all Muslims are brothers in virtue of their common religion, in spite of differences of race, language, and habitat. Now, in a world in which distance has been 'annihilated' by the progress of Western technology, and in which the Western way of life is having to compete with the Russian way of life for the allegiance of all mankind, the Islamic tradition of the brotherhood of Man would seem to be a better ideal for meeting the social need of the times than the Western tradition of sovereign independence for dozens of separate nationalities. In the new situation in which the Western community finds itself since the Second World War, its internal partition into about forty sovereign independent national states is threatening to bring about the fall of a house divided against itself. And yet the prestige of the West in the world is still high enough to make the Western virus of Nationalism still infectious. It is to be hoped that, in the Islamic world at any rate, the spread of this Western political malady may be arrested by the strength of a traditional Islamic feeling for unity. A world-wide political and social unity is necessary for us men and for our salvation today, in an atomic age, far more urgently than it has been in the past.

The Turkish people, under Atatürk's inspiration, have certainly done a service to the whole Islamic world in trying to solve a common 'Western Question' by adopting the modern Western way of life without reservations—Western Nationalism and all. But the other Islamic countries need not necessarily follow precisely the trail that these Turkish pioneers have blazed.

There are the Arabic-speaking Muslim countries, for instance, in which a common language is spoken in different dialects, but is written in one single standard literary language, from the Atlantic coast of Morocco to the western borders of Persia, and from Aleppo and Mosul on the north to Khartum and Aden and Maskat and Zanzibar on the south. Books and newspapers published in Cairo and Damascus and Beyrout circulate all over this huge Arabic-reading area and beyond it —for Arabic is the language of religion even in Islamic countries where it is not the language of everyday life. Is it really necessary that the Arabic-speaking world should break up—as the former

Spanish Empire in the Americas has so unfortunately broken up—into about twenty mutually
independent national states living in so many
water-tight compartments on the Western pattern? This is a seamy side of our Western civilization which it would surely be a pity for the Arabic-
speaking peoples to copy exactly.

And then, on all the fringes of the Islamic world
—in Tropical Africa, India, China, and the Soviet
Union—there are Muslim minorities—scattered
abroad among non-Muslim majorities—who will
never be able to gather all their members together
into geographically compact blocks capable of
forming so many sovereign independent states.
These scattered Muslim communities—which
amount to many millions of people all told—are
not, as we shall see, the only communities of the
kind; and, for all scattered communities like these,
the gospel of Western Nationalism spells, as we
shall find, not a call to a new life but a con-
demnation to death. Take the case of the great
Muslim community that is scattered over the face
of the sub-continent of India. In 1947, when Great
Britain withdrew from India, the Western spirit
of Nationalism unfortunately did not follow the
good example set by the human representatives of
the particular Western nation that had introduced
this Western ideology into India. Our Western
Nationalism stayed on in India, after the former

British administrators' departure, to split a previously united sub-continent into two bickering
successor-states—a Hindu Indian Union and a
Muslim Pakistan—and for both of them this split
has surely been a misfortune. The Indian Union is
something less than a united India; Pakistan is a
country composed of two fragments divided from
one another by the whole breadth of the Indian
Union; and, even after this jigsaw work, millions
of Hindus and Indian Muslims have found themselves living on the wrong side of the new frontiers
and have been faced with the cruel choice of leaving their homes or else falling under the rule of a
government that is not going to love them.

The Pakistanis do now possess a national state
of their own, and it is a large and a populous one.
But these Indian Muslims have had to pay a
higher price for this than the Turks, and a much
higher price than the Egyptians. They have dis-
covered, from experience, both the cost of our
Western Nationalism and its drawbacks. So the
Pakistanis, as well as the Turks, have been learning political lessons that are going to be valuable,
not only for other Islamic peoples, but also for the
world as a whole.

III

INDIA AND THE WEST

I<small>N</small> India's encounter with the West there has been one experience that has not been shared with India by any other society in the world. India is a whole world in herself; she is a society of the same magnitude as our Western society; and she is the one great non-Western society that has been, not merely attacked and hit, but overrun and conquered outright by Western arms, and not merely conquered by Western arms but ruled, after that, by Western administrators. In Bengal this Western rule lasted for nearly two hundred years, and in the Panjab for more than a hundred. India's experience of the West has thus been more painful and more humiliating than China's or Turkey's, and much more so than Russia's or Japan's; but, just for this reason, it has been also much more intimate. Personal contacts between Indians and Westerners have been more numerous, and our Western iron has probably entered deeper into India's soul.

Perhaps India would not have been conquered by Western arms if she had not been conquered by Muslim arms first. The reader has already been reminded that the Mughal last wave of Muslim conquerors of India overland arrived in India not many years after the first landing in India, in 1498, of the Portuguese first wave of Western mariners. These Mughal Muslims forestalled the British Westerners in bringing almost the whole of India under a single government. The Mughal peace in India may not have been so effective as the subsequent British peace was to be at its zenith; but the Mughal peace lasted as long as the British peace was to last, and, when, in the eighteenth century, it fell to pieces, it left legacies that made it not so difficult for the Mughals' British successors to reassemble the fragments of the Mughal Empire. One legacy was an imperial land-revenue organization which ran on by its own momentum during the eighteenth-century bout of anarchy in India. It ran on because it had become an Indian habit, and the conditioning of Indian hearts and minds to acquiesce, by force of habit, in an empire imposed on India by alien conquerors was the second of the Mughal legacies from which the Mughals' British successors profited.

The British successors of the Mughal rulers of India condemned their own revival of the Mughal rāj to come to an end when, in the eighteen-thirties, they deliberately set out to change the habits that their Mughal predecessors had implanted in Indian minds. In the eighteen-thirties the British rulers of India opened a window to the West for Indian minds by substituting a Western for an

Islamic and a Hindu higher education in India
and thereby introducing the Indians to their
British rulers' own Western ideas of liberty, parliamentary constitutional government, and Nationalism. The Indians took this Western political
education to heart. It moved them to demand for
India, and eventually moved the British to concede
to India, the self-government that Great Britain
enjoys; and today the Hindu successors of the
British rāj in the Indian Union, and the Muslim
successors of the British rāj in Pakistan, are dedi-
cated to the enterprise of ruling their shares of the
sub-continent on the lines on which their British
predecessors in the government of India have been
conducting the government of Great Britain since
1688.

It is perhaps particularly noteworthy that the
present Hindu rulers of the greater part of the
Indian sub-continent should have chosen, as they
have, to carry on the Government on Western
lines originally laid down by alien conquerors. In
the territories included in the Indian Union, the
Hindus are now masters in their own house for the
first time since the beginning of the Muslim conquest of India eight or nine hundred years ago. In
the eighteenth century, when the Mughal Muslim
rāj was breaking up, there were moments when it
looked as if it was going to be followed immediately
by the establishment of Hindu successor-states. In

he eighteenth-century scramble for the Mughals'
heritage, a Marāthā Hindu Power seemed for a
time to be well on the way to winning the lion's
share of the spoils. This eighteenth-century attempt
to transform the Mughal rāj into a Marāthā
Hindu rāj was foiled by the intervention of a more
powerful Western hand. But the establishment of
a British rāj instead of a Marāthā rāj did not
bring to a halt the resurgence of the Hindus in
their homeland. When the military line taken by
the Hindu renaissance in the eighteenth century
ended in a military failure, the gathering stream
of Hindu energy was merely diverted into a different channel. Under the British rāj in the nineteenth and twentieth centuries, as during the
interregnum in the eighteenth century, the Hindus
continued steadily to gain power in India, but
under the British régime they gained it, not by
force of arms, but by force of mastering a Western
system of education, administration and law which
were so many keys to power in a Westernizing
world.

The Hindus were quicker than the Indian
Muslims to see and seize the opportunity that, in
a Western age of Indian history, was open to
Indians who effectively cultivated the Western
arts of peace. Unlike the Indian Muslims, the
Hindus had no enervating memories of recently
lost power and glory to keep them brooding

ineffectively over a dead past instead of reaching out into the future; and so a balance of power which had begun to incline against the Muslims in an anarchic eighteenth century continued to go against them in the nineteenth and twentieth centuries under a British peace which set a premium on intellectual ability, in place of military prowess, as the qualification for advancement in the continuing competition between Hindus and Indian Muslims who were now alike subjects of a Western Crown. The Indian Muslims did, of course, eventually follow their Hindu fellow Indians' example. They, too, set themselves to master the arts of our Western civilization. Yet, when the voluntary liquidation of the British rāj in India came within sight, the Indian Muslims insisted that the retransfer of the Government of India from British to Indian hands must be accompanied by a partition of India between a Hindu and a Muslim successor state; and this insistence on separation was, in effect, a recognition of the truth that, since the days of 'the Great Moguls', there had been a reversal of the balance of power between Muslims and Hindus in India to the Muslims' disadvantage. In a joint Hindu–Muslim state including the whole sub-continent, the Indian Muslims feared that they would now be swamped by the Hindu majority of the population.

Though in 1947 a predominantly Muslim

Pakistan thus parted company with a predominantly Hindu Indian Union, the objective of the British Indian Empire's two successor-states has so far been the same. In this first chapter of their histories, the power in both states has been in the hands of the element in their population that has had a Western education and that has been inspired by this with Western ideals. If this element remains in power in India and Pakistan, as well as in Ceylon, we may look forward to seeing the statesmen of these Asian countries use their influence over their countrymen to persuade them to remain members of our 'free world'. No doubt these same Asian statesmen will continue to demand that, in a 'free world' that is to be the common home of Western and Asian peoples, there shall be no unfair and invidious discrimination against the Asian members of the family, and we Western members are bound to give satisfaction to our Asian fellow members on this point if, in calling our world 'free', we are sincere. Unless we Western members of 'the free world' grievously fail to live up to our professed liberal principles, we may hope to see the present Western-trained and Western-minded rulers of India, Pakistan, and Ceylon continue in partnership with us.

It is one of the vital interests of the Western peoples that this partnership of ours with the peoples of the Indian sub-continent should be

preserved; for these Indian peoples together constitute one of the two Asian quarters of the human
race; and, only two years after Great Britain had
made a move for the reconciliation of Asia with the
West by completing the liquidation of British rule
in Ceylon, Pakistan, the Indian Union, and Burma,
the Chinese, who constitute the second of the two
Asian quarters of the human race, went over from
the Western camp to the Russian. If after thus
losing the friendship of the Chinese sub-continent,
our Western world were to lose the friendship of
the Indian sub-continent as well, the West would
have lost to Russia most of the Old World except
for a pair of bridgeheads in Western Europe and
Africa; and this might well be a decisive event in
the struggle for power between 'the free world' and
Communism. The Indian Union—the successor-
state of the British Empire which covers most of the
Indian sub-continent, and the state in which the
Hindus are predominant—occupies a command-
ing position in the divided world of today, in
which the United States and her associates are
competing for world power with the Soviet Union
and her associates. In which direction is the Hindu
fifth of the human race going to incline? Let us
look at some of the considerations telling for and
against the likelihood of the Hindus continuing to
go our Western way.

Let us take a promising point first. It looks as if,

today, personal relations between Indians and Westerners are more friendly than they have ever been. Many citizens of the United Kingdom will certainly have had the experience—which the writer has had a number of times since 1947—of being surprised and touched by the friendliness that Indians have been going out of their way to show to British people. This has happened to the writer several times in foreign countries, where local observers were on the lookout to see what the relations between the Indians and the British really were now; and he has found Indians in conspicuous positions abroad going out of their way to show that the former unhappy estrangement between them and the British was now dead and buried as far as they were concerned. When Great Britain did completely fulfil her promise to liquidate her rule in India, the Indians were, it seems, taken aback. They had perhaps never fully believed that the British intended ever to fulfil their promises to India; and so, when the British did keep their word, there was a revulsion of feeling on the Indian side from hostility to friendliness. It is handsome of the Indians to make their new friendliness towards the British apparent; and this happy change in the relations of the Indians and the British with one another is assuredly something gained for our 'free world' as a whole.

The estrangement between India and a Western world which, for India, has been represented by Great Britain goes back behind the beginning of the Indian movement for independence in the eighteen-nineties, and behind the tragic conflict in 1857. It goes back to the reforms in the British administration in India that were started in the seventeen-eighties. This birth of estrangement from reform in the relations between Indians and British people is one of the ironies of history; and yet there is a genuine inner connexion between the two events. In the eighteenth century the then newly installed British rulers of India were free and easy with their newly acquired Indian subjects in two senses. They were unscrupulous in using their political power to fleece and oppress them, and at the same time they were uninhibited in their social relations with them. They hob-nobbed with their Indian subjects off duty, besides meeting them at work on less agreeable terms. The more intellectual British residents in India in the eighteenth century enjoyed the game of capping Persian verses with Indian colleagues; the more lively Indians enjoyed being initiated into English sports. Look at Zoffany's picture 'Colonel Mordaunt's Cock Match at Lucknow', painted in 1786. It tells one at a glance that, at that date, Indians and Englishmen could be hail-fellow-well-met with one another. The British rulers of India in the first generation behaved, in fact, very much as their Hindu and Muslim predecessors had behaved. They were humanly corrupt and therefore not inhumanly aloof; and the British reformers of British rule, who were rightly determined to stamp out the corruption and who were notably successful in this difficult undertaking, deliberately stamped out the familiarity as well, because they held that the British could not be induced to be superhumanly upright and just in their dealings with their Indian subjects without being made to feel and behave as if they were tin gods set on pedestals high and dry above those Indian human beings down below.

Today, when the Indians are once more governing themselves, so that Lord Cornwallis's problem of finding how to make Western administrators in India behave decently no longer arises, there is nothing to prevent the relations between Indians and Westerners from being intimate and decent at the same time, and this is a promising change for the better as far as it goes. But just how far does it go? After all, so few thousands out of India's 450 millions ever did or do meet a Westerner—or even meet a member of that Western-minded minority of the Indian people that is now governing India in the former Western rulers' place. And what is the future of this new Indian governing class? Will it be able to maintain its present leadership? And will the Western outlook and ideals, that have been implanted in the souls of this minority by their education, be able to hold their own, even here, against the Hindu tradition?

It is remarkable that even a minority in the great Hindu world should have gone so far as this now ruling minority has gone in assimilating Western ideas and ideals, considering how alien the Western and Hindu outlooks on life are from one another. In the two first chapters, in which we were concerned with Russia's and Islam's relations with the West, we were dealing with two cases in which the non-Western party with whom the West had collided had something in common with the West which Hinduism does not possess. Though our Russian contemporaries are not the children of Western Christians, they are the children of Eastern Orthodox Christians; and so both the Christian religion and also the Graeco-Roman civilization—which the Christian Church has taken over and preserved and handed down— are parts of the Russians' spiritual background, as they are parts of ours in the West. Our Muslim contemporaries, again, are adherents of a religion which, like Communism, can be described as being a Christian heresy; and the philosophy and science of the Greeks are parts of the Muslims' spiritual background, as they are of ours. In fact, if, looking at the contemporary world as a whole, one were to try to make the broadest and simplest analysis of the main cultural divisions in it, one would find oneself grouping the Muslims, the ex-Eastern Orthodox Christians and the ex-Western Christians together as members of a single great society which one could distinguish from both the Indian world and the Far Eastern world by giving this society, like each of those, an overall label of its own. Since the spiritual possession that all we Christians and Muslims have in common with one another is a pair of common heritages—one from the Jews and another from the Greeks—we could label our Christian-Muslim society the Graeco-Judaic, to distinguish it both from a Hindu Society in India and from a Confucian-Buddhist Society in the Far East.

From this bird's-eye view that takes in the whole of mankind, the divers Muslim and Christian variations on a common Graeco-Judaic way of life fade almost out of view. They look quite insignificant by comparison with the characteristics that are common to all of us Muslim and Christian members of our Graeco-Judaic cultural family. When we contrast our Muslim-Christian way of life as a whole with the Hindu way or with the Far Eastern, the differences, inside our Muslim-Christian family, between Eastern Orthodox Christendom and Western Christendom, or between either of these Christendoms and Islam, almost cease to be visible. And yet we know that these relatively small cultural differences can produce violent spiritual disturbances in the souls of the children of one of these Graeco-Judaic sister-civilizations of ours when these souls are played upon by the spiritual radiation of one of the other civilizations in our family.

A notable example is the effect produced on Russian souls by the impact on them of the Western civilization since the time of Peter the Great. The two parties to this encounter were, both of them, members of the same Graeco-Judaic family; yet the disturbance produced in Russian Graeco-Judaic souls by the strangeness of the intruding Western variety of the same Graeco-Judaic spirit has been very great. We can measure the severity of this disturbance psychologically by the tormented and tormenting vein in a nineteenth-century Russian literature which expresses, and gives vent to, the distress suffered by a soul when it is required to live in two different spiritual universes at once—even when these two claimants on the same soul's spiritual allegiance are rather closely akin to one another. We can also measure the severity of the Western stress and strain upon Russian souls politically by the explosiveness of the revolution in which this spiritual tension discharged itself in 1917.

Now the disturbance, produced by the impact of

the West on Russian souls, which has come to the surface in these sensational manifestations, is presumably a good deal milder than the latent disturbance produced in Indian souls by the same alien Western spiritual force; for the disturbance in Russian souls, violent though it has been, must have been mitigated by the presence, in Russia's cultural heritage, of Jewish and Greek elements that were also present in the heritage of the intruding Western civilization, whereas in the Indian heritage there have been no Greek or Jewish elements, or at any rate none to speak of, to break the force of the shock administered by the impact of the West here. What, then, in India, is going to be the resolution of this presumably far sharper tension between a native and an alien spiritual force? On the surface, those Hindus who have adopted our, to them, extremely alien Western culture on the planes of technology and science, language and literature, administration and law, appear to have been more successful than the Russians in harmonizing with their native way of life a Western way that is intrinsically more alien to them than it is to the Russians. Yet the tension in Hindu souls must be extreme, and sooner or later it must find some means of discharging itself.

Whatever may be the relief that Hindu souls are going to find for themselves eventually, it seems clear that, for them, there can be no relief from the impact of our Western civilization by opening themselves to the influence of Communism; for Communism—a Western heresy adopted by an ex-Orthodox Christian Russia—is just as much part and parcel of the Graeco-Judaic heritage as the Western way of life is, and the whole of this cultural tradition is alien to the Hindu spirit.

There is, however, one factor in the economic and social situation in India today which might give Communism an opening—exotic though Communism may be in a Hindu environment— and this subversive factor is the rising pressure of population in India on the means of subsistence. This is an important point, because the same factor is at work today in China, Japan, Indo-China, Indonesia, and Egypt. In all these non-Western countries the impact of the West has brought with it a progressive increase in the food supply through irrigation, through the introduction of new crops, and through the improvement in methods of agriculture under Western inspiration; and in all of them, at every stage so far, this increase in the food supply has been spent, not on raising the standard of living of a stationary or gradually growing population, but on maintaining the largest possible population on the old level, which was and is only just above starvation point. Since progressive improvements in productivity must sooner or later bring in diminishing returns, the standard of this swollen population seems bound to decline, and there is no margin between the present standard and sheer disaster on the grand scale.

In some such economically desperate situation as this, Communism might win a foothold in India and in other Asian countries in which Communism is just as foreign as our Western way of life. For Communism has a programme of wholesale compulsory collectivization and mechanization to offer as a specious remedy for the plight of a depressed Asian peasantry, whereas, to people in this plight, it would be a mockery to advise them to solve their problem in the American way. This population problem, and its bearing on the competition between Russia and the West, will confront us again when we come to the Far East, which is the subject of the next chapter.

IV

THE FAR EAST AND THE WEST

IN the last chapter it was suggested that our Western way of life was more foreign to the Hindus than it was to the Russians and the Muslims, because the Hindu way had in it no more than a minute dose of the Greek and Jewish ingredients that are the common heritage of Islam, Russia, and the West. The Far East has still less in common with the West than the Hindu world has in its cultural background. It is true that in Far Eastern art the influence of Greek art is noticeable; but this Greek influence reached the Far East through an Indian channel; it came in the train of an Indian religion—Buddhism—which captured the Far Eastern world as the Graeco-Roman world was captured by a Judaic religion, Christianity. It is also true that another Judaic religion— Islam—which spread over the greater part of India by conquest, also spread over the western fringes of China by peaceful penetration. Thus the Far East, like India, had already been played upon by influences from our Graeco-Judaic world before it was assaulted by our modern Western civilization in the sixteenth century; but in the Far East these pre-Western Graeco-Judaic influences had been even slighter than they had been in India. They had been too slight to pave the way for the kindred Western civilization's advent. And so, when in the sixteenth century the Portuguese pioneers of the Western civilization made their first landfalls on the coasts of China and Japan, they descended there like uncanny visitants from some other planet.

The effect of this first modern Western visitation on the Far Eastern peoples' feelings was mixed. It was an unstable mixture of fascination and repulsion, and, at this first encounter, the feeling of repulsion finally prevailed. This sixteenth-century wave of Western intruders was thrown back into the Ocean out of which it had broken so unexpectedly upon Far Eastern shores; and, after that, Japan, Korea, and China each closed her doors and set herself, as long as she could, to live as 'a hermit kingdom'. This, however, was not the end of the story. After the modern Western intruders had been expelled from Japan in the seventeenth century and from China in the eighteenth century, they returned to the charge in the nineteenth century; and, at this second attempt, they succeeded in introducing the Western way of life into the Far East, as by then they had already introduced it into Russia and India and were beginning to introduce it into the Islamic world.

What differences in the situation can we see that will account for the difference in the result of these two successive Western attempts to captivate the Far East?

One obvious difference is a technological one. In the sixteenth and seventeenth centuries, Western ships and weapons were not so decisively superior to Far Eastern ships and weapons as to give the Western intruders the whip hand. In this first round in the encounter between the two civilizations, the Far Easterners remained masters of the situation; and, when they decided that they wanted to break the relation off, their Western visitants were powerless to resist. But, when the Westerners reappeared off the coasts of China and Japan in the nineteenth century, the weight was in the Western scale of the balance of power; for, while Chinese and Japanese armaments were then still what they had been two hundred years back, the Westerners had made the industrial revolution in the meantime; they now came back armed with new-fangled weapons which the Far Eastern Powers could not match; and, in these new circumstances, the Far East was bound to be opened to Western influences in one or the other of two ways. A Far Eastern hermit kingdom that tried to meet the new technological challenge from the West by ignoring it would soon see its closed doors battered in by Western heavy guns. The only alternative was to keep the Western intruders at arm's length by learning the 'know-how' of nineteenth-century Western armaments; and this could only be done by voluntarily opening Far Eastern doors to the new Western technology before an entry was forced by Western conquerors. The Japanese were prompter than the Chinese in opting for, and acting on, this alternative policy of holding their own against the West by learning how to use and make the latest types of Western weapons; but the Chinese, too, in the end, acted just in time to save themselves from India's fate of being subjugated by a Western Power.

This, though, is not the whole story. For, while the technological ascendancy gained by the West over the Far East through a Western industrial revolution may explain why the Far Eastern peoples found themselves compelled to open their doors to the Western civilization in the nineteenth century, we have still to explain why they had been moved to expel their Western visitants and to break off relations with the Western world in the seventeenth and eighteenth centuries. This denouement of the first encounter between the Far East and the modern West is at first sight surprising; for, when the Westerners had made their first appearance above the Far Easterners' horizon in the sixteenth century, the Far Eastern peoples had shown themselves readier to welcome these then quite unknown strangers and to adopt their way of life than they showed themselves three hundred

years later, when the Westerners came again with
the bad reputation that they had acquired on
their first visit. Yet this second encounter, in which
the Far Eastern peoples were decidedly reluctant to
engage, ended in the reception of the Western way
of life in the Far East, whereas the first encounter,
which had begun with a welcome, had ended in a
rebuff. What is the key to this remarkable difference between these two acts in the drama of the
Far East's encounter with the West?

The difference in the Far Eastern peoples' reaction to the Western civilization on these two
occasions was not arbitrary or capricious. They
reacted differently because the challenges with
which they were confronted on the two occasions
were not the same. In the nineteenth century the
Western civilization presented itself primarily as a
strange technology; in the sixteenth century it had
presented itself primarily as a strange religion.
This difference in the aspect displayed by the intrusive Western civilization explains the difference
in the reaction that it aroused in Far Eastern hearts
and minds at its first and at its second coming; for
a strange technology is not so difficult to accept as
a strange religion is.

Technology operates on the surface of life, and
therefore it seems practicable to adopt a foreign
technology without putting oneself in danger of
ceasing to be able to call one's soul one's own.

This notion that, in adopting a foreign technology, one is incurring only a limited liability may, of course, be a miscalculation. The truth seems to be that all the different elements in a culture-pattern have an inner connexion with each other, so that, if one abandons one's own traditional technology and adopts a foreign technology instead, the effect of this change on the technological surface of life will not remain confined to the surface, but will gradually work its way down to the depths till the whole of one's traditional culture has been undermined and the whole of the foreign culture has been given entry, bit by bit, through the gap made in the outer ring of one's cultural defences by the foreign technology's entering wedge.

In China and Korea and Japan today, a century or more after the date at which our modern Western technology first began to penetrate these countries, we can see these revolutionary ulterior effects upon the whole of their culture taking place before our eyes. Time, however, is of the essence of this process; and a revolutionary result that is so clearly manifest to all eyes today was not foreseen by Far Eastern statesmen a hundred years ago, when they were reluctantly taking their decision to admit this foreign technology within their walls. Like their Turkish contemporaries, they intended to take the West's technology in the minimum dose required for their own military security, and not to go beyond that. Yet, even if they had had some suspicion of the hidden forces that this mechanically propelled Trojan Horse held in ambush within its iron frame, probably they would still have stood by their decision to wheel it in. For they saw clearly that, if they hesitated to adopt this alien Western technology now, they would immediately become a prey to Western conquerors armed with weapons to which they would then have no retort. The external danger of conquest by some Western Power was the immediate menace with which those nineteenth-century Far Eastern statesmen had to cope. By comparison, the internal danger of being eventually captivated, body and soul, by the Western way of life as a result of adopting the Western technology was a more distant menace which must be left to take care of itself. Sufficient unto the day is the evil thereof.

Thus, in the nineteenth century, the adoption of a now overwhelmingly superior Western technology appeared to Far Eastern statesmen to be a legitimate risk as well as an imperative necessity. And this explains why, this time, they took something from the West which was so little to their taste. It seemed to be at any rate a lesser evil than the alternative of being conquered and subjugated by the Westerners whose weapons they were deciding to adopt as a policy of military and political insurance. On the other hand, the 'Western Question' with which these nineteenth-century Far Eastern statesmen's seventeenth-century predecessors had had to deal had presented itself in quite a different form.

In this first encounter with the West the immediate danger which Japanese statesmen had to parry was not the danger of seeing their country conquered by Western soldiers armed with irresistibly superior new-fangled weapons; it was the danger of seeing their people converted by Western missionaries preaching an irresistibly attractive foreign religion. Possibly these seventeenth-century Japanese statesmen had no great objection to Western Christianity in itself; for, unlike their seventeenth-century Western Christian visitants, seventeenth-century Far Easterners were not infected with the religious fanaticism which their Western contemporaries had inherited from Christianity's Jewish past and were displaying, in this age, in domestic religious wars in their European homeland. The Chinese and Japanese statesmen of the day had been brought up in the more tolerant philosophical traditions of Confucianism and Buddhism, and they might not have objected to giving a free field to another religion if they had not suspected the Western Christian missionaries' religious activities of having an ulterior political motive.

What the Japanese statesmen feared was that

their countrymen whom these foreign missionaries were converting to Western Christianity would imbibe their adopted religion's fanatical spirit, and that, under this demoralizing influence, they would allow themselves to be used as what, in the West today, we should call 'a fifth column'. If this suspected design were to succeed, then Portuguese or Spaniards, who in themselves were not a serious menace to Japan's independence, might eventually contrive to conquer Japan through the arms of Japanese traitors. In fact, the Japanese Government in the seventeenth century outlawed and repressed Christianity from the same motive that today is moving twentieth-century Western governments to outlaw and repress Communism; and it has been an element that is common to these two Western faiths—the fanaticism inherited by both of them from Judaism—that has been the stumbling-block in any Asian country in which Christianity has been propagated.

An aggressive foreign religion will, in fact, manifestly be a more serious immediate menace than an aggressive foreign technology will be to a society that it is assailing; and there is a deeper reason for this than the danger of the converts being used as 'a fifth column'. The deeper reason is that, while technology plays only upon the surface of life in the first instance, religion goes straight down to the roots; and, though a foreign technology, too, may eventually have a deeply disintegrating effect on the spiritual life of a society in which it has once gained a footing, this effect will take some time to make itself apparent. For this reason, an aggressive civilization that presents itself as a religion is likely to arouse stronger and swifter opposition than one that presents itself as a technology; and we can now see why in the Far East, as well as in Russia, our Western civilization was first rejected and was then accepted at the second time of asking. In Russia in the fifteenth century and in the Far East in the seventeenth century, the Western civilization was rejected when what it was demanding was conversion to the Western form of Christianity; and it was no accident that its fortunes in the mission field should have veered right round from conspicuous failures to sensational successes as soon as its attitude towards its own ancestral religion had veered round from a warm devotion to a cool scepticism.

This great spiritual revolution overtook the Western world towards the close of the seventeenth century, when a hundred years' trial of waging savage and inconclusive civil wars under the colours of rival religious sects had at last disgusted the Western peoples, not only with wars of religion, but with religion itself. The Western world reacted to this dissillusioning self-inflicted experience of the evils of religious fanaticism by withdrawing its treasure from religion and reinvesting it in technology; and it is this utilitarian technological excerpt from the bible of our Western civilization, with the fanatical religious page torn out, that has run like wildfire round the world during the last two and a half centuries, from the generation of Peter the Great to the generation of Mustafā Kemāl Atatürk.

Perhaps, in looking for some explanation of the striking difference between the results of the West's two successive assaults upon the Far East, we have stumbled upon a 'law' (if one may call it that) which applies, not just to this single case, but to all encounters between any civilizations. This 'law' is to the effect that a fragment of a culture, split off from the whole and radiated abroad by itself, is likely to meet with less resistance, and therefore likely to travel faster and farther, than the culture as a whole when this is radiated *en bloc*. Our Western technology, divorced from our Western Christianity, has been accepted, not only in China and Japan, but also in Russia and in many other non-Western countries where it was rejected so long as it was offered as part and parcel of a one and indivisible way of life including Western Christianity as well.

The almost world-wide dissemination of a technological splinter flaked off from our Western civilization since the close of the seventeenth century is impressive at first sight if we compare it with the virtual failure to convert non-Western peoples to the Western way of life in an Early Modern Age when our Western civilization was being offered for acceptance or rejection as a whole—technology, religion and all. Today, however, when the West's bid to win the world has been challenged by Russia, we can see that our Western civilization's apparent triumph on the technological plane is precarious for the very reason that has made it easy; and the reason is that this triumph has been superficial. The West has sent its technology racing round the world by the trick of freeing it from the handicap of being coupled with our Western Christianity; but, in the next chapter of the story, this unattached Western technology has been picked up by the Russians and been coupled with Communism; and this new and potent combination of a Western technology with a Western religious heresy is now being offered to the Far Eastern peoples and to the rest of mankind as a rival way of life to ours.

In the nineteenth-century chapter of the story, we Westerners were gratified when we saw the Japanese and the Chinese, who had rejected our Western civilization in its religious version, accepting it in a secularized version in which technology instead of religion had been given the place of honour. The Meiji Revolution in Japan in the eighteen-sixties and the Kuomintang Revolution in China in the nineteen-twenties both seemed, at the time, to be triumphs for the secularized Western civilization of the Late Modern Age. But we have lived to see this secular Western dispensation disappoint us in both countries. In Japan it bred a disastrous militarism; in China it bred a disastrous political corruption; in both countries the disaster brought the régime to a violent end; and in China this failure of the attempt to acclimatize there a secular form of our Western civilization has been followed by a victory for Communism. What is it that has made Communism's fortune in China? Not, so far as one can make out, any great positive enthusiasm for Communism so much as a complete disillusionment with the Kuomintang's performance in its attempt to govern China on latter-day secular Western lines. And we may suspect that the Japanese too, if they were free to go their own way, might succumb to Communism for the same negative reason.

In both Japan and China today there are two factors telling in Communism's favour: first, this disillusionment with past experiments in trying to lead a secularized Western way of life, and, second, the pressure of a rapidly growing population on the means of subsistence—a pressure which, as has been noticed in the preceding chapter, is also a menace to the present Westernizing régime in India. The truth is that, in offering the Chinese and Japanese a secularized version of our Western civilization, we have been offering them a stone instead of bread, while the Russians, in offering them Communism as well as technology, have been offering them bread of a sort—gritty black bread, if you like to call it so; but that is still an edible substance that contains in it some grain of nutriment for the spiritual life without which Man cannot live.

But, if China and Japan could not stomach a sixteenth-century version of our Western civilization with the religion left in, and cannot sustain life on a nineteenth-century version of it with the religion left out, is Communism the only alternative? The answer to this question is that, in China, and also in India, in the sixteenth and seventeenth centuries, long before Communism was ever dreamed of, a different alternative *was* found and tried by the Jesuit Western Christian missionaries. It is true that this experiment came to grief, but it was wrecked, not by any intrinsic faults of its own, but by unfortunate rivalries and dissensions between the Jesuits and other Roman Catholic Christian missionary orders.

In China and India the Jesuits did not make the mistake, that they had made in Japan, of letting their preaching of Christianity fall under suspicion of being conducted in the political interests of aggressive Western Powers. The Jesuits' approach to their enterprise of propagating Christianity in China was so different and so promising in itself, and is so much to the point today, that our discussion of the Asian peoples' encounter with the West would be incomplete if we did not take into consideration the line which the Jesuits in China and India opened out. Instead of trying, as we have been trying since their day, to disengage a secular version of the Western civilization from Christianity, the Jesuits tried to disengage Christianity from the non-Christian ingredients in the Western civilization and to present Christianity to the Hindus and to the Chinese, not as the local religion of the West, but as a universal religion with a message for all mankind. The Jesuits stripped Christianity of its accidental and irrelevant Western accessories, and offered the essence of it to China in a Chinese, and to India in a Hindu, intellectual and literary dress in which there was no incongruous Western embroidery to jar on Asian sensibilities. This experiment miscarried at the first attempt through the fault of domestic feuds within the bosom of the Roman Catholic Church of the day, which had nothing to do with either Christianity or China or India; but, considering that India and China and Christianity are all still on the map, we may expect—and hope—to see the experiment tried again. The recent victory of Communism in China over a Western civilization divorced from Christianity is no evidence that, in China, Christianity has no future in a coming chapter of history which today is still below our historical horizon.

V

THE PSYCHOLOGY OF ENCOUNTERS

IN the first four chapters of this book we have been surveying four episodes in which our Western civilization has been encountered by some contemporary non-Western society. Russia's, Islam's, India's, and the Far East's experiences of the West have come under view. Our survey has shown that these four different experiences of being hit by a foreign civilization have had a number of features in common; and the purpose of the present chapter is to pick out, for further examination, several features that appear to be characteristic, not only of the contemporary world's encounters with the West, but of all such collisions between one civilization and another. There seems to be something like a common psychology of encounters; and this is a subject of practical interest and importance today, when the sudden 'annihilation of distance', through the achievements of our Western technology, has brought face to face, at point-blank range, half a dozen societies, each of which, until yesterday, was living its own life in its own way almost as independently of its neighbours as if each society had been marooned on a planet of its own instead of living in the same world with the other representatives of its kind.

We may begin by reminding ourselves of a general phenomenon which came to our notice in the last chapter when we were taking a comparative view of our Western civilization's two successive assaults upon China and Japan. We saw that, on the first occasion, the West tried to induce the Far Eastern peoples to adopt the Western way of life in its entirety, including its religion as well as its technology, and that this attempt did not succeed. And then we saw that, in the second act of the play, the West offered to the same Far Eastern peoples a secularized excerpt from the Western civilization in which religion had been left out and technology, instead of religion, had been made the central feature; and we observed that this technological splinter, which had been flaked off from the religious core of our civilization towards the end of the seventeenth century, did succeed in pushing its way into the life of a Far Eastern Society that had previously repulsed an attempt to introduce the Western way of life *en bloc*—technology and all, including religion.

Here we have an example of something that seems often to happen when the culture-ray of a radioactive civilization hits a foreign body social. The assaulted foreign body's resistance diffracts the culture-ray into its component strands, just as a light-ray is diffracted into the spectrum by the resistance of a prism. In optics we also know that some of the light-strands in the spectrum have a greater penetrative power than others, and we have already seen that it is the same with the component strands of a culture-ray. In the West's impact on the Far East, the technological strand in the radiation of the Western civilization has overcome a resistance by which the religious strand has been repelled; and this difference in the penetrative power of a religious and a technological culture-strand is not a phenomenon that is peculiar to the history of the relations between these two particular civilizations. We have stumbled here upon an instance of one of the 'laws' of cultural radiation.

When a travelling culture-ray is diffracted into its component strands—technology, religion, politics, art, and so on—by the resistance of a foreign body social upon which it has impinged, its technological strand is apt to penetrate faster and farther than its religious strand; and this law can be formulated in more general terms. We can say that the penetrative power of a strand of cultural radiation is usually in inverse ratio to this strand's cultural value. A trivial strand arouses less resistance in the assaulted body social than is aroused by a crucial strand, because the trivial strand does not threaten to cause so violent or so painful a disturbance of the assaulted body's traditional way of life. This automatic selection of the most trivial elements in a radioactive culture for the widest dissemination abroad is obviously an unfortunate rule of the game of cultural intercourse; but this premium on triviality is not the game's worst point. The very process of diffraction, which is of the essence of the game, threatens to poison the life of the society whose body social is being penetrated by the divers strands of a diffracted culture-ray.

Analogies taken from physics and medicine may be used to illustrate this point. Since our discovery of the trick of splitting the atom, we have learnt to our cost that the particles composing an atom of some inoffensive element cease to be innocuous and become dangerously corrosive so soon as they have been split off from the orderly society of particles of which an atom is constituted, and have been sent flying by themselves on independent careers of their own. We have learnt, too—not to our own cost in this case, but to the cost of the once secluded surviving representatives of Primitive Man—that a disease which is a mild one for us, because it has been rife among us so long that we have developed an effective resistance to it, may prove deadly to South Sea Islanders who have been exempt from it before being suddenly exposed to it by the arrival among them of its European carriers.

A loose strand of cultural radiation, like a loose electron or a loose contagious disease, may prove deadly when it is disengaged from the system within which it has been functioning hitherto and is set free to range abroad by itself in a different milieu. In its original setting, this culture-strand or bacillus or electron was restrained from working havoc because it was kept in order by its association with other components of a pattern in which the divers participants were in equilibrium. In escaping from its original setting, the liberated particle, bacillus, or culture-strand will not have changed its nature; but the same nature will produce a deadly effect, instead of a harmless one, now that the creature has broken loose from its original associations. In these circumstances, 'one man's meat' can become 'another man's poison'.

In the set of encounters between the world and the West which is the subject of this book, there is a classical example of the mischief that an institution can do when it is prised loose from its original social setting and is sent out into the world, conquering and to conquer, all by itself. During the last century and a half we have seen our Late Modern Western political institution of 'national states' burst the bounds of its birthplace in Western Europe and blaze a trail of persecution, eviction, and massacre as it has spread abroad into Eastern Europe, South-West Asia, and India—all of them regions where 'national states' were not part and parcel of an indigenous social system but were an exotic institution which was deliberately imported from the West, not because it had been found by experimentation to be suitable to the local conditions of these non-Western worlds, but simply because the West's political power had given the West's political institutions an irrational yet irresistible prestige in non-Western eyes.

The havoc which the application of this Western institution of 'national states' has worked in these regions where it is an exotic import is incomparably greater than the damage that the same institution has done in Britain, France, and the other West European countries in which it has been, not an artificially introduced innovation, but a spontaneous native growth.

We can see why the same institution has had strikingly different effects in these two different social environments. The institution of 'national states' has been comparatively harmless in Western Europe for the same reason that accounts for its having originated there; and that is because, in Western Europe, it corresponds to the local relation between the distribution of languages and the alinement of political frontiers. In Western Europe, people speaking the same language happen, in most cases, to be huddled together in a single continuous and compact block of territory with a fairly well defined linguistic boundary separating it from the similarly compact domains of other languages; and, in a region where, as here, the languages are thus distributed in the pattern of a patchwork quilt, the linguistic map provides a convenient basis for the political map, and 'national states' are therefore natural products of the social milieu. Most of the domains of the historic states of Western Europe do, in fact, coincide approximately with homogeneous patches of the linguistic map; and this coincidence has come about, for the most part, undesignedly. The West European peoples have not been acutely conscious of the process by which their political containers have been moulded on linguistic lasts; and, accordingly, the spirit of nationalism has been, on the whole, easy-going in its West European homeland. In West European national states, linguistic minorities who have found themselves on the wrong side of a political frontier have in most cases shown loyalty, and been treated with consideration, because their coexistence with the majority speaking 'the national language' as fellow citizens of the same commonwealth has been an historical fact which has not been deliberately brought about by anyone and which has therefore been taken for granted by everyone.

But now let us consider what has happened when this West European institution of 'national states', which in its birthplace has been a natural product of the local linguistic map, has been radiated abroad into regions in which the local linguistic map is on a quite different pattern. When we look at a linguistic map, not just of Western Europe, but of the world, we see that the local West European pattern, in which the languages are distributed in fairly clear-cut, compact, and homogeneous blocks, is something rather peculiar and exceptional. In the vastly larger area stretching south-eastward from Danzig and Trieste to Calcutta and Singapore, the pattern of the linguistic map is not like a patchwork quilt; it is like a shot-silk robe. In Eastern Europe, South-West Asia, India, and Malaya the speakers of different languages are not neatly sorted out from one another, as they are in Western Europe; they are geographically intermingled in alternate houses on the same streets of the same towns and villages; and, in this different, and more normal, social setting, the linguistic map—in which the threads of different colours are interwoven with each other —provides a convenient basis, not for the drawing of frontiers between states, but for the allocation of occupations and trades among individuals.

In the Ottoman Empire, a hundred and fifty years ago, before the Western institution of clear-cut, compact, homogeneous national states made its disastrous entry into this foreign arena, the

Turks were peasants and administrators, the Lazes were sailors, the Greeks were sailors and shopkeepers, the Armenians were bankers and shopkeepers, the Bulgars were grooms and market-gardeners, the Albanians were masons and mercenary soldiers, the Kurds were shepherds and porters, the Vlachs were shepherds and pedlars. The nationalities were not only intermingled as a matter of geographical fact; they were also economically and socially interdependent; and this correspondence between nationalities and occupations was the order of nature in a world in which the linguistic map was, not a patchwork, but a macédoine. In this Ottoman world the only way of carving out national states on the Western pattern was to transform the native macédoine into a patchwork on the linguistic pattern of Western Europe; and this could be done only by the methods of barbarism which, for a hundred and fifty years past, have in fact been employed with devastating results in one section after another of an area extending all the way from the Sudetenland to Eastern Bengal. So great can be the havoc worked by an idea or institution or technique when it is cut loose from its original setting and is radiated abroad, by itself, into a social environment in which it conflicts with the historic local pattern of social life.

The truth is that every historic culture-pattern

is an organic whole in which all the parts are inter-dependent, so that, if any part is prised out of its setting, both the isolated part and the mutilated whole behave differently from their behaviour when the pattern is intact. This is why 'one man's meat' can be 'another man's poison'; and another consequence is that 'one thing leads to another'. If a splinter is flaked off from one culture and is introduced into a foreign body social, this isolated splinter will tend to draw in after it, into the foreign body in which it has lodged, the other component elements of the social system in which this splinter is at home and from which it has been forcibly and unnaturally detached. The broken pattern tends to reconstitute itself in a foreign environment into which one of its components has once found its way.

If we want to see how, in the game of cultural intercourse, this process of one thing leading to another works in practice, let us look at one or two concrete examples.

In a United Kingdom blue book surveying the social and economic state of Egypt in 1839, it is mentioned that, in the city of Alexandria at this date, the principal maternity hospital is located within the precincts of the naval arsenal. This sounds odd, but we shall see that it was inevitable as soon as we retrace the sequence of events that led to this at first sight surprising result.

By the year 1839 the Ottoman governor-general of Egypt, the celebrated Mehmed 'Alī Pasha, had been working for thirty-two years to equip himself with effective armaments in the Western style of his generation. The failure of Napoleon's expedition to Egypt had opened Mehmed 'Ali's eyes to the importance of sea-power. He was determined to have a navy composed of warships on the contemporary Western model; he realized that he would not be navally self-sufficient till he was in a position to have Egyptian warships built in an Egyptian naval dockyard by Egyptian hands; and he also realized that he could not provide himself with an Egyptian personnel of naval technicians without hiring Western naval architects and other experts to train his Egyptian apprentices. So Mehmed 'Ali advertised for Western experts; and suitable Western candidates were tempted to apply for these jobs in Egypt by the handsome scale of pay that the Pasha was offering. All the same, these Western applicants were unwilling to sign their contracts without being sure of being able to bring their families to Egypt with them; and they were unwilling to bring their families without being sure of there being suitable provision for the care of their health up to contemporary Western standards of medical service. So Mehmed 'Ali found that he could not hire his urgently required Western naval experts without also hiring Western doctors of medicine to attend on the naval experts' wives and children; and, as his heart was set on his ambition to create an Egyptian navy, he did hire the doctors as well. Doctors and experts and their families all arrived from the West together; the experts duly installed the arsenal and the doctors duly attended on the women and children in the new Western community at Alexandria; but, when the doctors had done all their duty by their Western patients, they found that they still had some working time on their hands; and, being the energetic and public-spirited medical practitioners that they were, they resolved to do something for the local Egyptian population as well. With what should they begin? Maternity work was obviously the first call. So a maternity hospital arose within the precincts of the naval arsenal by a train of events which, as you will now recognize, was inevitable.

The moral of this story is the speed with which, in cultural intercourse, one thing can lead to another, and the revolutionary length to which the process may go. Within the lifetime of all concerned, the traditional seclusion of Muslim women from contact with men outside their own household had still been so strictly enforced that in eighteenth-century Turkey, even when one of the Sultan's most dearly beloved wives was so ill that her life was in danger, the most that the

Islamic code of manners would allow a Western doctor to do for this precious imperial patient was just to feel the pulse of a hand held out timidly between the tightly drawn curtains of the invisible lady's bed. This was the nearest that a Western physician had been permitted to approach a patient whose life was one of the principal treasures of a ruler who was deemed to be an autocrat. In those days the Sultan's autocracy had been impotent to override a traditional Islamic social convention, even in a matter of life and death which was next to the so-called autocrat's heart. And now, within the same lifetime, Muslim women were boldly venturing inside the precincts of an outlandish arsenal to avail themselves of the services of infidel Western obstetricians. This dire breach with the traditional Islamic conceptions of decency in the social relations between the sexes had been a consequence of the Pasha of Egypt's decision to equip himself with a navy in the Western style; and this undesigned and, at first sight, remote social effect had followed its technological cause within the span of less than half a lifetime.

This piece of social history, which is piquant but not unrepresentative, gives the measure of the degree to which those nineteenth-century Ottoman statesmen were deluding themselves when they imagined that they would be able to fit their country out with adequate Western armaments and then to arrest the process of Westernization at that point. It was not till the time of Mustafā Kemāl Atatürk, in our own day, that the 'Osmanlis admitted to themselves the truth that, in the game of cultural intercourse, one thing is bound to go on leading to another until the adoption of Western weapons, drill, and uniforms will inevitably bring in its train not only the emancipation of Muslim women but the replacement of the Arabic by the Latin alphabet and the disestablishment of an Islamic Church which, in Muslim countries in the past, has reigned unchallenged over the whole field of life.

In our own day in India, President Atatürk's great Hindu contemporary the Mahatma Gandhi did realize that in cultural intercourse one thing insidiously leads to another. Gandhi saw that a myriad threads of cotton—grown in India, perhaps, but spun in Lancashire and woven there into clothes for India's people—were threatening to entangle India with the Western world in gossamer meshes that might soon be as hard to break as if they had been steel fetters. Gandhi saw that, if Hindus went on wearing clothes made by Western machinery in the West, they would soon take to using the same Western machinery in India for the same purpose. First they would import jennies and power-looms from England; then they would learn how to build these implements for themselves; next they would be leaving their fields in order to work in their new Indian cotton-mills and Indian foundries; and, when they had become used to spending their working-time doing Western jobs, they would take to spending their leisure on Western amusements—movies, talkies, greyhound racing, and the rest—till they would find themselves growing Western souls and forgetting how to be Hindus. With a prophet's vision the Mahatma saw this grain of cotton-seed waxing into a great tree whose spreading branches would overshadow a continent; and this Hindu prophet called upon his Hindu countrymen to save their Hindu souls by laying an axe to this rank Western tree's roots. He set them the example of spending a certain time every day on spinning and weaving Indian cotton by hand, in the old-fashioned Indian way, for Indian bodies to wear, because he saw that this severance of the germinal economic ties between India and the West was the only sure means of saving the Hindu society from going Western, body and soul.

There was no flaw in the Mahatma Gandhi's insight. The Westernization of India that he foreboded and sought to avert was, and is, fast developing out of that one original grain of cotton-seed; and Gandhi's remedy for India's Western infection was the right one. Only the prophet failed to induce his disciples to follow him in preserving India's cultural independence at this price in economic austerity. The wearing of machine-made cotton goods could not have been renounced by the Indian people in Gandhi's generation without lowering the Indian peasantry's already intolerably low standard of living, and without putting out of business altogether the new classes of Indian cotton operatives and Indian mill-owners that had already sprung up from India's soil in Bombay and in Gandhi's own native city, Ahmadabad. Gandhi has made an immense and perhaps permanent mark on the history of India and of the world; but the irony of history has condemned him to make this mark, not by saving India from economic Westernization, but by speeding her along the path of political Westernization through leading her triumphantly to the Western political goal of national self-government. Even Gandhi's genius was no match for the remorseless working of a social 'law'. In a cultural encounter, one thing inexorably goes on leading to another when once the smallest breach has been made in the assaulted society's defences.

Our inquiry will have made it evident that the reception of a foreign culture is a painful as well as a hazardous undertaking; and the victim's instinctive repugnance to innovations that threaten to upset his traditional way of life makes the experience all the worse for him; for, by kicking against the pricks, he diffracts the impinging foreign culture-ray into its component strands; he then gives a grudging admission to the most trivial, and therefore least upsetting, of these poisonous splinters of a foreign way of life, in the hope of being able to get off with no further concessions than just that; and then, as one thing inevitably leads to another, he finds himself compelled to admit the rest of the intruding culture piecemeal. No wonder that the victim's normal attitude towards an intrusive alien culture is a self-defeating attitude of opposition and hostility.

In the course of our survey we have had occasion to notice some of the statesmen in non-Western countries hit by the West who have had the rare vision to see that a society which is under fire from the radiation of a more potent foreign culture must either master this foreign way of life or perish. The figures of Peter the Great, Selīm III, Mahmūd II, Mehmed 'Alī, Mustafā Kemāl, and 'the Elder Statesmen' of Japan in the Meiji Era have passed before our eyes. This positive and constructive response to the challenge of cultural aggression is a proof of statesmanship because it is a victory over natural inclinations. The natural response is the negative one of the oyster who closes his shell, the tortoise who withdraws into his carapace, the hedgehog who rolls himself up into a spiky ball, or the ostrich who hides his head in the sand, and there are classical examples of this alternative reaction in the histories of both Russia's and Islam's encounters with the West.

The policy of learning how to fight an aggressive alien civilization with its own weapons will arouse deep misgivings in conservative minds. Are not your Peters and your Mustafā Kemāls really selling the fort under pretext of bringing its defences up to date? Is not the right retort to the intrusion of an alien culture a resolute determination to boycott the accursed thing? If we scrupulously obey every jot and tittle of the holy law that has been laid upon us by the God of our fathers, will He not be moved to put forth the almighty power of His right arm for our defence against our infidel enemies? In Russia this was the reaction of the Old Believers, who suffered martyrdom for the sake of minute, and in foreign eyes trifling, points of ecclesiastical ritual; and in the Islamic world this was the reaction of the Wahhābīs, Sanūsīs, Idrīsīs, Mahdists, and other puritanical sects who came charging out of the desert on God's war-path against apostate 'Osmanlis, who, in the fanatics' eyes, had betrayed Islam by going the Western way.

Muhammad Ahmad, the Sudanese fanatic, is the antithesis of Peter the Russian technocrat; but neither the mastering of a new-fangled alien technology nor a zeal for the preservation of a traditional way of life is the last word in reply to the challenge of an assaulting alien civilization. If we are to read what this last word is, we must look ahead to a chapter of the story which, in the unfinished history of the world's encounter with the West, is today still hidden in the future. We can supply this missing chapter if we turn to the history of the world's encounter with the Greeks and Romans; for, in the record of this episode, the scroll of history has already been unrolled from beginning to end, so that the whole of this older book now lies open for our inspection. Our future can perhaps be deciphered in this record of a Graeco-Roman past. Let us see what we can make of this Graeco-Roman record.

VI

THE WORLD AND THE GREEKS AND ROMANS

O NE of the besetting infirmities of living creatures is egotism, as we all know from personal experience; and in self-conscious creatures this self-centredness generates an illusion. Every soul, tribe, and sect believes itself to be a chosen vessel; and the falsity of our belief in our own unique value does not easily become apparent to us. We can see the fallacy readily, though, when it is a case of somebody else hugging this illusion about himself. We Westerners, being human, are inclined to feel that what we have done to the world within the last few centuries is something unprecedented. An effective cure for this Western illusion of ours is to glance back at what, not so very long ago, was done to the world by the Greeks and Romans. We shall find that they too overran the world in their day, and that they too believed for a time that they were not as other men are. We shall also find, before we come to the end of this story of the world's encounter with the Greeks and Romans, that, in this episode, a temporarily dominant Graeco-Roman society's estimate of its own value broke down under the test of being weighed in the truth-finding balance of history.

The expansion of the West over the world which

began with our dramatically sudden conquest of the oceans at the end of the fifteenth century has its counterpart in Graeco-Roman history in the expansion of the Greek world overland in and after the generation of Alexander the Great in the fourth century B.C. Alexander's march across Asia from the Dardanelles to the Panjab made as revolutionary a change in the balance of power in the world as the voyages of Da Gama and Columbus; and, like these, it was followed up by wider conquests in later generations. In the second century B.C. the Greeks conquered India right across to Bengal, and in the same century the Romans won for the Graeco-Roman world a frontage on the Atlantic Ocean in what are now Southern Spain and Portugal. The Basic Greek in which the New Testament was written in the first century of the Christian Era was spoken and understood from Travancore to the hinterland of Marseilles. At the same date Britain was being annexed to the Graeco-Roman world by force of Roman arms, while Greek art in the service of an Indian religion —Buddhism—was travelling peacefully northeastwards from Afghanistan along a road that was eventually to carry it across China and down Korea to Japan. Thus, in sheer physical range, the Graeco-Roman culture, in its day, spread as widely in the Old World as our Western culture has spread in its day; and, in an age which had not

yet seen the emergence of the indigenous civilizations of the Americas, the Greeks could boast, as
we can today, that every contemporary civilization on the face of the planet (whose shape and size
the Greeks had accurately calculated) had been
reached and penetrated by the radiation of their
world-conquering culture.

This impact of a Greek culture on the world in
and after the fourth century B.C. gave the world as
sharp a shock as the impact of our modern Western
culture has been giving it since the fifteenth century
of our era; and, as human nature has not under-
gone any perceptible change within the last few
thousand years, it is not surprising to find the
standard alternative psychological reactions to a
cultural assault, which we have observed in the
history of the world's encounter with ourselves,
making their appearance likewise in the history of
the world's earlier encounter with the Greeks and
Romans.

This passage of history, too, can muster its in-
transigent mahdis and its adaptable Peter the
Greats. In Peter's line, for example, there was
Mithradates the Great, an Iranian king in Asia
Minor, who very nearly got the better of the
Romans by arming and drilling his troops in the
Greek and Roman style and by taking the field
against Rome as a rival patron and champion of
the Greeks and their culture. And there was Herod

the Great, the Edomite King of Judaea, who was worsted by Psyche's task. Herod's self-assigned mission was to educate his stiff-necked Palestinian Jewish subjects into acquiescing in the minimum compromises with Greek civilization and with Roman power which, for a small Oriental people in a predominantly Graeco-Roman world, were the only practical alternatives to the desperate course of provoking and incurring annihilation. The Herodian policy of prudent accommodation to imperious historical facts was defeated by the obstinacy of a long line of Palestinian Jewish mahdis. This militant movement had begun in the second century B.C. in a fierce revolt against the Hellenizing policy of a Greek King of south-west Asia. Anyone re-reading the First and Second Books of Maccabees will almost certainly be struck by the family likeness between the Maccabees' insurrection in Palestine in 166–165 B.C. and the Mahdi Muhammad Ahmad's insurrection in the Egyptian Sudan in A.D. 1881. After flickering up again in the insurrections of a Theudas and a Judas whose signal failures are cited by Gamaliel in the Acts of the Apostles, the flame of this fanatical Palestinian Jewish resistance to Hellenism rose to its final flare in the second century of the Christian Era in the revolt of Bar Kōkabā, who proclaimed himself the Messiah and was crushed by the Roman Emperor Hadrian.

These Palestinian Jewish leaders of an Oriental resistance movement to the Graeco-Roman civilization were not the only representatives of their kind. Already before the end of the third century B.C. there had been something like an 'Indian Mutiny' among native Egyptian troops who had been armed and drilled in the Greek style by a Greek King of Egypt for the defence of his dominions against an invasion by a South-West Asian Greek contemporary of his. The Greek-drilled Egyptians routed the full-blooded Greek troops in the invading army; and their astonishing victory over descendants of Alexander's invincible soldiers went to these native Egyptian soldiers' heads. And then there were outbreaks among the most ill-fated of all the Orientals who had fallen under Greek or Roman rule—the Syrians who had been kidnapped and been deported overseas to work as slaves in chain-gangs on Greek plantations in Sicily. Before the end of the second century B.C. these Syrian slaves in Sicily had made two desperate insurrections against their Greek masters and these masters' Roman protectors.

This grim tale of cruel oppression and savage revolt in the earlier chapters of the history of the world's encounter with the Greeks and Romans has found echoes in familiar chapters of the parallel history of the world's encounter with the West. In a Westernized world the slave-trade that once

disgraced the Mediterranean has been revived in
the Atlantic; the insurrection of plantation-slaves
that was crushed in Sicily has been victorious in
Haiti; the mutiny of the Ptolemies' Greek-drilled
native Egyptian troops has been matched by the
mutiny of a British East India Company's Western-
drilled sepoys; and militant Oriental resistance
movements against an alien ascendancy, that are
reminiscent of the unsuccessful anti-Hellenic insurrections of the Palestinian Jews and the successful anti-Hellenic insurrections of the contemporary
Iranian peoples, are in full swing at this moment
in Indo-China and Malaya and are threatening to
break out at three places in Africa. Up to this point
we can read the story in our own record without
needing to consult the Greeks' and Romans'
dossier. But now we are reaching and passing the
point where, on the open page of our book, the
moving finger is writing in the latest entries in our
still unclosed account; and, beyond this point,
where the curtain veils our own future, the Graeco-
Roman account is our best source of potential
information about what may be in store for us.

Of course I am not meaning to suggest that we
can cast a horoscope of our own future by observ-
ing what happened in Graeco-Roman history
beyond this point, where our own record breaks
off, and then mechanically translating this
Graeco-Roman record into modern Western

terms. History does not automatically repeat itself; and the most that any Graeco-Roman oracle
can do for us is to reveal one among a number
of alternative possible future denouements of our
own drama. In our case the chances may well be
against the plot's working out to its Graeco-Roman
conclusion. It is conceivable that we Westerners
and our non-Western contemporaries may give
the course of our encounter with each other some
quite different turn which has no counterpart in
Graeco-Roman history. In peering into the future
we are fumbling in the dark, and we must be on
our guard against imagining that we can map out
the hidden road ahead. All the same, it would be
foolish not to make the most of any glimmer of
light that hovers before our eyes; and the light
reflected upon our future by the mirror of past
Graeco-Roman history is at any rate the most
illuminating gleam that is visible to us.

With these counsels of caution in our minds, let
us now go on turning the pages of the book of
Graeco-Roman history till we come to the picture
of the Graeco-Roman world half-way through the
second century after Christ. When we compare this
with the picture of the same world two hundred
years earlier, we shall perceive at once that in the
interval there has been a change for the better
here which unfortunately has had no parallel in
our Western history up to date. In the last century

B.C. the Graeco-Roman world had been racked by revolutions, wars, and rumours of wars, and had been seething with tumult and violence, quite as feverishly as our Western world is today; but midway through the second century after Christ we find peace reigning from the Ganges to the Tyne. The whole of this vast area, stretching from India to Britain, through which the Graeco-Roman civilization has been propagated by force of arms, is now divided between no more than three states, and these three are managing to live side by side with a minimum of friction. The Roman Empire round the shores of the Mediterranean, the Parthian Empire in 'Irāq and Iran, and the Kushan Empire in Central Asia, Afghanistan and Hindustan, cover the whole of the 'Graeco-Roman world between them; and, though the makers and masters of these three empires are all non-Greek in origin, they are nevertheless all 'Philhellenes', as they are proud to call themselves: that is to say, they consider it to be their duty and their privilege to foster the Greek form of culture and to cherish the self-governing municipalities in which this Greek way of life is being kept alive.

Let us look into the hearts and minds of the millions of Greeks and Romans and the many more millions of Hellenized and semi-Hellenized ex-Orientals and ex-barbarians who are living under the shelter of a second-century Roman-

Parthian-Kushan peace. The waters of war and revolution which had gone over the souls of this generation's great-great-grandparents have now ebbed away, and the nightmare of that time of troubles has long since ceased to be a living memory. Social life has been stabilized by constructive statesmanship; and, though the settlement has fallen far short of the ideals of social justice, it is tolerable even for the peasantry and the proletariat, while for all classes it is indisputably preferable to the Ishmaelitish anarchy to which it has put a long overdue end. Life now is more secure than it was in the preceding age; but for this very reason it is also more dull. Like humane anaesthetists, a Caesar and an Arsaces and a Kanishka have taken the sting out of those once burning economic and political questions that, in a now already half-forgotten past, were the salt as well as the bane of human life. The benevolent action of efficient authoritarian governments has undesignedly created a spiritual vacuum in human souls.

How is this spiritual vacuum going to be filled? That is the grand question in the Graeco-Roman world in the second century after Christ; but the sophisticated civil servants and philosophers are still unaware that any such question is on the agenda. The people who have read the signs of the times and have taken action in the light of these indications are the obscure missionaries of half-a-dozen Oriental religions. In the long-drawn-out encounter between the world and the Greeks and Romans, these preachers of strange religions have gently stolen the initiative out of Greek and Roman hands—so gently that those hard hands have felt no touch and, so far, have taken no alarm. Yet, all the same, the tide has turned in the Greeks' and Romans' trial of strength with the world. The Graeco-Roman offensive has spent its force; a counter-offensive is on its way; but this counter-movement is not yet recognized for what it is, because it is being launched on a different plane. The offensive has been military, political, and economic; the counter-offensive is religious. This new religious movement has before it a prodigious future, as time is going to show. What are the secrets of its coming success? There are three on which we can put our finger.

One factor that, in the second century after Christ, is favouring the rise and spread of the new religions is a weariness of the clash of cultures. We have watched the Orientals responding to the challenge of a radioactive Greek culture along two antithetical lines. There have been statesmen of Herod the Great's school, whose prescription for living in a Graeco-Roman cultural climate has been to acclimatize oneself, and there have been fanatics whose prescription has been to ignore the change of climate and to go on behaving as though this change had not occurred. After an exhaustive trial of both these strategies, fanaticism has discredited itself by turning out to be disastrous, while the Herodian policy has discredited itself by turning out to be unsatisfying. Whichever of the two alternative strategies has been followed, this cultural warfare has led nowhere; and the moral of this anticlimax is that no single human culture can make good its conceited claim to be a spiritual talisman. Disillusioned minds and disappointed hearts are now ready for a gospel that will rise above these barren cultural claims and counterclaims. And here is the opportunity for a new society, in which there shall be neither Scythian nor Jew nor Greek, neither bond nor free, neither male nor female, but in which all shall be one in Christ Jesus—or in Mithras, Cybele, Isis, or one of the bodhisattvas, an Amitabha or perhaps an Avalokita.

An ideal of human fraternity that will overcome the clash of cultures is thus the first secret of the new religions' success, and the second secret is that these new societies, which are open to all human beings, with no discrimination between cultures, classes, or sexes, also bring their human members into a saving fellowship with a superhuman being; for the lesson that human nature without God's grace is not enough has by now been graven deep on the hearts of a generation that has seen the tragedy of a time of troubles followed by the irony of an oecumenical peace.

At least two breeds of human gods have now been tried and been found wanting. The deified militarist has been a flagrant scandal. Alexander, as the Tyrrhenian pirate told him to his face in the story as we have it from Saint Augustine, would have been called not a god but a gangster if he had done what he did with a couple of accomplices instead of doing it with a whole army. And what about the deified policeman? Augustus, now, has made himself into a policeman by liquidating all his fellow gangsters, and we are grateful to him for that; but, when we are required to register our gratitude by worshipping this reformed gangster as a god, we cannot comply with much conviction or enthusiasm; and yet our hearts are hungry for a divinity that we can worship in spirit and in truth.

In the gods who have made their epiphany in the new religions, we are at last in the presence of divinities to whom we can devote ourselves with all our heart and mind and strength. Mithras will lead us as our captain. Isis will nurse us as our mother. Christ has emptied Himself of His divine power and glory to become incarnate as a man and to suffer death upon the cross for our sake. And for our sake likewise a bodhisattva who has reached the threshold of Nirvāna has refrained from taking the last step into bliss. This heroic pathfinder has deliberately condemned himself to go on haunting the sorrowful treadmill of existence for aeons upon aeons more; and he has made this extreme sacrifice for the love of fellow sentient beings whose feet he can guide into the way of salvation so long as he pays the huge price of himself remaining sentient and suffering.

These were the appeals of the new religions to a majority of mankind who, in the Graeco-Roman world in the age of the imperial peace, were weary and heavy laden—as indeed they are at all times and places. But what about the Greek and Roman dominant minority that had devastated the world by conquering and plundering it, and were now patrolling the ruins as self-commissioned gendarmes? 'They make a desert and call it peace' is the verdict on their handiwork that one of their own men of letters has put into the mouth of one of their barbarian victims. How were sophisticated and cynical Greek and Roman masters of the world going to respond to the challenge of the world's counter-offensive on the religious plane which was the world's answer to its rulers' previous offensive on the plane of war and politics?

If we look into these Greek and Roman hearts in the generation of Marcus Aurelius, we find a spiritual vacuum here also; for these earlier

conquerors of the world, like us their present
Western counterparts, had long ago discarded their
ancestral religion. The way of life which they had
chosen for themselves, and had been offering to all
Orientals and barbarians whom they had brought
within the range of Greek cultural influence, was
a secular way in which the intellect had been con-
scripted to do duty for the heart by working out
philosophies that were to take religion's place.
These philosophies, which were to have set the
mind free, had bound the soul to the sorrowful
wheel of natural law. 'Up and down, to and fro,
round and round: this', the philosopher-emperor
Marcus confessed to himself, 'is the monotonous
and meaningless rhythm of the Universe. A man
of average intelligence who has arrived at the age
of forty years will have experienced everything
that has been and is and is to come.'

This disillusioned Greek and Roman dominant
minority was, in fact, suffering from the same
spiritual starvation as the majority of contemporary mankind, but the new religions which were
now being offered to all men and women without
respect of persons would have stuck in a philo-
sopher's throat if the missionary had not sugared
the strange pill for him; and so, for the sake of
accomplishing their last and hardest task of converting a Greek-educated die-hard core of a pagan
public, the new religions did clothe themselves in

divers forms of Greek dress. All of them, from Buddhism to Christianity inclusive, presented themselves visually in a Greek style of art, and Christianity took the further step of presenting itself intellectually in terms of Greek philosophy.

This, then, was the last chapter in the history of the world's encounter with the Greeks and Romans. After the Greeks and Romans had conquered the world by force of arms, the world took its conquerors captive by converting them to new religions which addressed their message to all human souls without discriminating between rulers and subjects or between Greeks, Orientals, and barbarians. Is something like this historic denouement of the Graeco-Roman story going to be written into the unfinished history of the world's encounter with the West? We cannot say, since we cannot foretell the future. We can only see that something which has actually happened once, in another episode of history, must at least be one of the possibilities that lie ahead of us.